This High School Musical
Annual belongs to

Catherine mary stuart

ANNUAL 2010
East High Forever!

First published in Great Britain 2009 by Egmont UK Limited, 239 Kensington High Street, London W8 6SA
Created for Egmont by John Brown. Editorial: Jayne Miller, Helen Ward. Design: Tim Clear, Tom Moore
HSM © 2009 Disney Enterprises Inc.
Based on the Disney Channel Original Movie "High School Musical," written by Peter Barsocchini
Based on the Disney Channel Original Movie "High School Musical 2," written by Peter Barsocchini
Based on the Disney Channel Original Movie "High School Musical 3: Senior Year," written by Peter Barsocchini
Based on the screenplay written by Peter Barsocchini
Based on characters created by Peter Barsocchini
Executive Producer Kenny Ortega
Produced by Bill Borden and Barry Rosenbush
Directed by Kenny Ortega
All rights reserved.

ISBN 978 1 4052 4650 7
3 5 7 9 10 8 6 4 2
Printed in Italy
Note to parents: Adult supervision is recommended for the crafts.

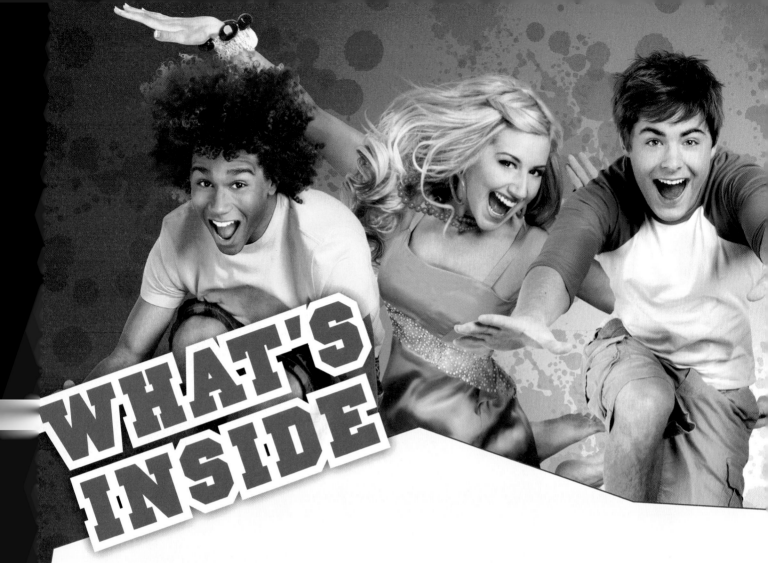

WHAT'S INSIDE

East High Forever!

MOST LIKELY TO

The future is full of possibilities! Write in what you think the students will be doing in five years' time!

GABRIELLA MONTEZ

One of the smartest students at East High. Not only is she a maths genius, but she also has an angelic voice, a sweet nature and the ability to get everybody together.

In five years' time Gabriella will be:

JASON CROSS

A good friend, a great basketball player and a very sincere and loyal person.

In five years' time Jason will be:

ZEKE BAYLOR

Top of the class for food tech and one of the top scorers on the basketball team. A winning combination!

In five years' time Zeke will be:

CHAD DANFORTH

Chad always aims high. He lives for basketball and his friends, and can't wait to wear

In five years' time Chad will be:

TROY BOLTON

Popular and multi-talented. He'll succeed in his chosen career – whatever it turns out to be!

In five years' time Troy will be:

SUCCEED

KELSI NIELSEN

Quietly and calmly composing the music for every musical. When will the spotlight shine on her?

In five years' time Kelsi will be:

MARTHA COX

Proving brainy girls make great cheerleaders. She has the moves and the maths.

In five years' time Martha will be:

RYAN EVANS

Never still, this natural mover will choreograph his trip to the top.

In five years' time Ryan will be:

TAYLOR MCKESSIE

Organised, efficient, supremely intelligent and totally into science. A future president maybe?

In five years' time Taylor will be:

SHARPAY EVANS

Sharpay's talent is matched by her ambition. Watch out Hollywood!

In five years' time Sharpay will be:

9

The cheerleaders are totally out of step! Can you put them in order to spell out the name of some high-school activities?

L A S T A B L E B K

1.

I T R F S | **I D A**

2.

E S H R Y M I T C

3.

M A R A D

4.

I E A N C H E D R E G L

5.

G O N K C I O

6.

DESIGN YOUR OWN WILDCATS T-SHIRT!

This supporters' banner is written in code. What are they trying to say?

Clue: Complete the code-cracker rosette first!

UGJBAYRQ FYTC QGVRCCL KGLSRCQ RM UGL!

10

TROY BOLTON:

EAST HIGH HIGHLIGHTS

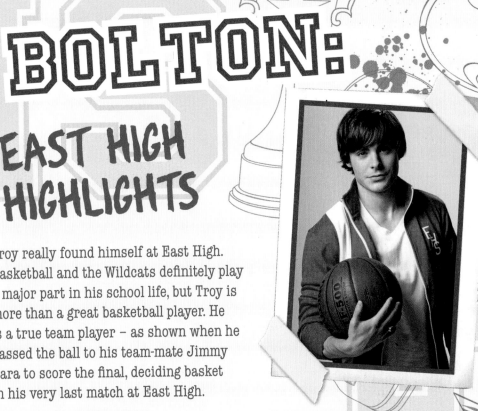

Troy really found himself at East High. Basketball and the Wildcats definitely play a major part in his school life, but Troy is more than a great basketball player. He is a true team player – as shown when he passed the ball to his team-mate Jimmy Zara to score the final, deciding basket in his very last match at East High.

Sporting highlights

Troy was the youngest East High student to make the basketball team when he joined. With Troy as captain and then as co-captain with Chad, the Wildcats had a wild winning streak!

Natural performer

Troy surprised everyone, including himself, by auditioning for the winter musical in the Junior Year. Then he and Gabriella got the star roles and he still managed to captain his basketball team when they won the State championships! That's two highlights in one week!

Once Troy found his singing voice, he discovered he was a natural performer, on the basketball court – and on stage! There was no going back!

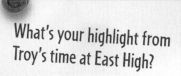

What's your highlight from Troy's time at East High?

....

....

11

AUDITIONS:

HOW TO ROCK THEM!

It's show time again. We're all getting ready for the Spring Musical, and this year everyone is going to audition – that includes you! Sign up, take some tips and fill in the notes to get your routine sorted!

SIGN UP FOR THE SHOW!

Sharpay

Ryan

Catherine

WRITE YOUR NAME HERE

LEARN YOUR LINES
Learn a new song by listening to it over and over. Then write down the lyrics and sing it alone!

MUSIC NOTES
OK, so first you need to choose a song ...
* Choose something to suit your voice, but don't be afraid to try something different.
* Perhaps you're more of a rock star or a rapper? Go for it!
* Then decide if you're gonna grab the limelight alone or dazzle the judges with a group effort.

MY SONG: *The LaZaSy*

SOLO ✓ DUET ◯ GROUP ◯

DANCE DOS 'N' DON'TS
Dancing can set your performance apart and help you relax and enjoy yourself!
* Don't make it too complicated, or there's more chance of it going wrong.
* Make use of the whole stage area! Don't keep your back to the audition panel!
* Practise! Especially if there's a group of you!

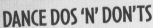

SOLO DANCE: ◯

GROUP DANCE: ◯

12

GET THE LOOK

You have just a few moments to wow your audience – make the most of them!

✳ The right outfit, shoes and hairdo can work wonders for you. Plan ahead!

✳ If you are performing with a pal or a group, get colour co-ordinated!

✳ Go OTT with a dressy suit or costume, or stick with street style if that fits your act.

DESIGN YOUR OUTFIT HERE:

SING IT LOUD!
Warm up your vocal chords by taking a deep breath and singing 'La' a few times, making the sound last longer each time.

MS. DARBUS' STAGE SCHOOL

Look comfortable up there!

✳ If you're not a natural dancer, sitting on a stool can stop you fidgeting or swaying as you sing.

✳ Like Gabriella, you may feel awkward at the thought of people staring at you, but try to look up and into the audience.

✳ Avoid looking at friends who give you the giggles!

PROP FOR ROUTINE:

STEP  UP!

When you're on stage, people notice your feet, so choose your footwear with care! Guess which East High performers these shoes belong to.

⑤

S h a r p y

③

T r o y

⑥

T a y l o r

①

G a b r e l u r

②

C H A D

④

G a b r e l u r

⑦

R a i n

WORDY WONDER!

Your gran may not look as cool as Troy, but they're just seven steps apart! Change Troy into gran by altering just one letter at a time.

TROY

	Carry your cups on one
	Don't be caught in one
	To the shops or up the stairs maybe?
	To hold tightly
	Another word for smile!

GRAN

D.I.Y. WORD LADDERS

Start with any five-letter word and take turns changing one letter at a time to create a new word. Pass it round a few times and see what you end up with!

• Start easy – turn smile into stage in just two steps... and take it from there!

Over to you!

SMILE

	Helps you climb over a wall
	When food goes off

STAGE

ANSWERS ON PAGE 67

Most Likely to Succeed!

YOUR TALENT SHOW TURN!

What will you do in the talent show? Go hip-hop, form a rock band, sing a starry solo – or maybe a tap dance is more your style? Try our fun flowchart and find out!

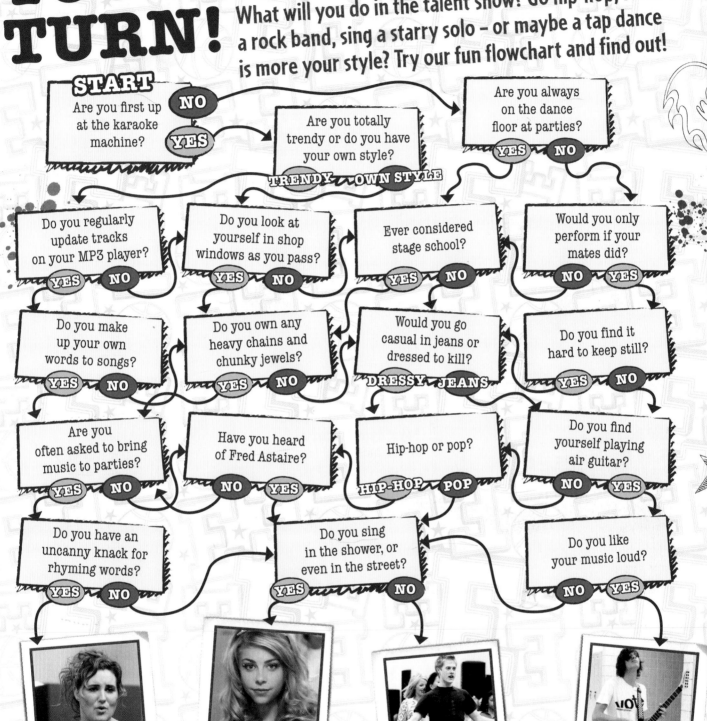

START
Are you first up at the karaoke machine? — NO / YES

Are you totally trendy or do you have your own style? — TRENDY / OWN STYLE

Are you always on the dance floor at parties? — YES / NO

Do you regularly update tracks on your MP3 player? — YES / NO

Do you look at yourself in shop windows as you pass? — YES / NO

Ever considered stage school? — YES / NO

Would you only perform if your mates did? — NO / YES

Do you make up your own words to songs? — YES / NO

Do you own any heavy chains and chunky jewels? — YES / NO

Would you go casual in jeans or dressed to kill? — DRESSY / JEANS

Do you find it hard to keep still? — YES / NO

Are you often asked to bring music to parties? — YES / NO

Have you heard of Fred Astaire? — NO / YES

Hip-hop or pop? — HIP-HOP / POP

Do you find yourself playing air guitar? — NO / YES

Do you have an uncanny knack for rhyming words? — YES / NO

Do you sing in the shower, or even in the street? — YES / NO

Do you like your music loud? — NO / YES

HAPPY HIP-HOPPER!
You love a good beat and enjoy dancing, but the words are what matter most to you. Performance is about the content and delivery rather than the costume and the show!

A STAR IS BORN!
You're not shy about stepping into the limelight. You love getting up and putting on a show – the bigger the audience, the better! Take the stage for a starry solo and earn that applause!

DANCING DUDE
You find it hard to keep still – your toes just keep tapping! Wow the crowd with your moves and grooves and you'll get everyone clapping along!

ROCK ON!
You're only comfortable on stage sharing the limelight with pals. Having a guitar or drums to play helps you concentrate on something other than the audience!

15

WHADDAYA KNOW?

Test your High School Musical knowledge right here!

1

Who does Ms. Darbus ask to help her run the Drama department next year?

a) Kelsi

b) Ryan

c) Sharpay

Answer [c]

2

What does Troy give Gabriella as a promise that they'll be together over the summer?

a) Leftover lemon cookies that Zeke baked for him earlier

b) A pendant wth 'T' on it

c) A Wildcats top with her name on it

Answer [b]

3

How does Mr. Evans arrive for his family game of golf?

a) By helicopter

b) In a flash convertible with a 'FABULUS' number plate

c) In a golf cart driven by Ryan

Answer [b]

4

How many 'Rules about Boys' does Taylor's sister have?

a) 10

b) 100

c) 13

Answer [ ]

5

What does Sharpay use her golf club as before she takes a swing?

a) A mirror

b) Something to hit Ryan with

c) A dancing prop

Answer [ ]

6

Troy and Gabriella have an evening picnic on the golf course. What does Sharpay order Mr. Fulton to do?

a) Ban all non-members from the golf course

b) Turn the sprinklers on

c) Make Troy her golf coach

Answer [ ]

16

8

Whose team wins the staff baseball game?

a) Chad's team

b) Ryan's team

c) No one wins because Sharpay interrupts the game and orders them to stop playing

Answer ☐

7

As assistant to the golf pros, what does Troy have to do for a job?

a) Clean all the golf pros' shoes

b) Teach golfers how to dance

c) Teach kids how to play golf

Answer ☐

9

How does Zeke store his game socks?

a) He stuffs them with cotton wool

b) He keeps them in the fridge

c) He vacuum seals them

Answer ☐

10

What colour is Sharpay's locker?

a) Silver

b) Pink

c) Gold

Answer

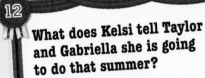

11

What is the name of Jimmie's cologne?

a) Eau d'Odour

b) Babe Magnet

c) Get the Girls

Answer ☐

12

What does Kelsi tell Taylor and Gabriella she is going to do that summer?

a) Learn how to play basketball

b) Grow and write music

c) Take up knitting

Answer ☐

13

Who becomes Sharpay's new personal assistant?

a) Troy

b) Tiara Gold

c) Zeke

Answer ☐

ANSWERS ON PAGE 67

CRAZY CROSSWORD!

Get your brain into gear with our cunning crossword!

(Grid answers visible: 1 Down — lifeguard)

CLUES

Across:

1. You do this at Chad's jokes!
4. Taylor was putting this school souvenir together
5. Kelsi's surname
8. What type of show did the East High crew put on?
9. The final year at East High
12. What does Troy call Kelsi?
13. Ms. Darbus teaches this
14. Group of people who play a sport
17. Sporty types wear them on their feet
19. What is Ryan good at?
21. She's head of the cheerleaders in Senior Year
22. Name of the first spring musical
23. See 16 down

Down:

1. Gabriella's summer job
2. Another team game the East High crew have played
3. What's Mr. Bolton known as?
6. Naughty students get this!
7. End-of-school party
10. What does Ryan like to practise?
11. What were Troy and Chad both before Troy was promoted to golf instructor?
15. If you want a show role you have to do this
16. **and 23 across** Name of the Evans' holiday resort
18. When the Wildcats succeed in a game, they are the ...
20. The theme for the East High prom is 'The Last _____'

ANSWERS ON PAGE 67

GABRIELLA MONTEZ:

EAST HIGH HIGHLIGHTS

East High was special for Gabriella – the first place where she wasn't just the 'freaky genius girl'. She finally felt like she fitted in and made lasting friends – and not just with the maths crowd!

Team triumph

Joining Taylor on the Scholastic Decathlon team was fun! With Gabriella's quick thinking, the team put East High on the map by beating their rivals in a huge showdown!

Musical moments

Who would have thought that shy Gabriella would get up and sing in front of a hall full of students – and an audience! It's amazing what you can do when people show that they believe in you!

Chemistry mix

Gabriella had a big effect on East High, too. She helped to get the little groups to mix – cheerleaders chatted to brainiacs, skate dudes hung out with basketball players and Gabriella was right in the middle of them all!

WHAT'S YOUR EAST HIGH HIGHLIGHT FOR GABRIELLA?

....

....

....

TEAM WORK:

PUTTING ON A SHOW!

If you don't fancy singing in public, join the team behind the scenes. Help design or paint the scenery, choose and create costumes, try choreography. Feel part of the show, even if you're not comfortable performing!

SCENIC ROUTE?

	yes	no
Do you enjoy painting?	✓	
Are you creative?	✓	✗
Can you draw?		
Do you know what two colours mix to make green?	✓	

If you answered yes to three or more, the **scenery** department needs you!

MUSIC MAESTRO PLEASE!

Someone has to organise the music – you? From choosing the tunes, playing instruments or getting the MP3 player to work, music is an essential part of the show. And what about finding sound effects, like creaky doors or loud footsteps, even a few screams?

MUSIC FOR MY SHOW
- ◯ BAND
- ◯ ORCHESTRA
- ◯ MP3

TECHY TALK

The performers steal the show, undoubtedly, but there would be nothing to see without the lights!

There is a long list of backstage jobs, including finding props and organisi timings and scene changes.

And on the other side of the stage - creating the posters, selling tickets publicising it ... what good is a sho without an audience?

SHOW SNAPPERS

Performers are not allowe to write their own reviews (luckily!). If you're good with a camera, snap up a job as a photographer, or write a review for the scho yearbook or web page!

WARDROBE WONDERS

Do you have a knack for choosing clothes that go well together?

Can you use a needle and thread?

Do you know what period costume is?

Maybe you have a way with wigs?

Costume designers, stylists and dressers are essential! Not all performers have Sharpay and Ryan's sense of style - most actors need a good costume department to make them look fab!

MY IDEAL BACKSTAGE JOB:

2

FANCY FOOTWORK

Put your best foot forward on or off court! Dig out an old pair of trainers or buy a pair of plain ones and create a unique look for your feet!

WHAT YOU NEED

- Pencil · Scissors · Paper
- Fabric paints in red/blue/glitter
- Pair of old plain trainers or plimsolls

GLITZY OPTIONS

- 12cm red sequin lace
- 2 red pompoms
- Needle and red thread OR fabric glue

TIP:
Choose an easy logo and draw it on cardboard first. Cut around it to create a template – unless you are a freestyle expert!

1 This is your blank canvas – start creating! Plan your design first. Once you use fabric paint, you won't be able to change it. Sketch your ideas on paper and try out colours on a fabric scrap.

2 Draw an outline. When you know what you want on your trainers, use a pencil to lightly sketch the different areas of your design. Start simply and add to your design as you go along.

CHEERLEADER STYLE
• Cut a length of lace or a sequin strip and stitch or glue it around the top of your trainer.

• Simple, glittery patterns work well with sequins!

TIP:
Don't forget the heel and back of your shoe. We've added a couple of shooting stars!

QUICK FIX
Changing the colour of your laces gives an instant lift to your shoes!

3

Colour the outline in first. Fabric pens are easiest for this, or use a thin-tipped paintbrush and fabric paint. Then colour inside the lines. Wait for this to dry if you are changing colours or adding glitter.

4

Use glitter fabric paints on top of your design to add sparkle, or paint over an entire area of your trainers in another colour. Sew a pompom to the end of each lace for a true designer touch!

GET'CHA HEAD IN

Take some sporting tips from the the Wildcats and improve your game – whatever it is!

FANCY FOOTWORK!

Keep on your toes! Whether it's gymnastics, basketball, volleyball or tennis you're playing, look lively! You'll find it's easier to turn and cover the court, and you're always ready to run (but not away from the ball!) You even look as if you're playing better! Try it!

KEEP YOUR HEAD IN THE GAME ...

You can't be in the action all the time. Even if the ball is up at the other end of the pitch or you're waiting for your turn, keep alert and always keep your eyes on the ball – and your opponents. You don't want to miss your opportunity to shine! Know where your team-mates are at all times. Team games are about working together.

SHOW COMMITMENT!

Always turn up for your training sessions, even if it's dark, cold and raining! Once you're with your friends, you'll be pleased you made the effort and you're more likely to get picked for the starting line-up. Besides, you probably need the practice!

TRUE OR FALSE!

Check your check list!

a) My sports/dance kit is always clean and packed ready to go! true ☐ false ☐

b) I know what I should eat before a match or training, and when. true ☐ false ☐

c) I pack a chocolate bar to eat at half time. true ☐ false ☐

d) I carry a skipping rope around with me everywhere. true ☐ false ☐

e) I rest a lot, watching TV every night after school. true ☐ false ☐

THE GAME

GO FOR IT!

You can't be half-hearted if you want to win! Budding sports stars don't have to carry a ball around at all times like Chad, but practise your sport whenever you can. Improve your fitness levels by jogging or cycling to school.

* Carry a skipping rope with you. You don't need anyone to help you skip, you can do it (almost) anywhere! It's fantastic all-round excercise.

A WORD FROM THE COACH!

Listen to your coach! You may think you know better, but coaches can stand back and look at the whole game – you can't! If you're a captain, don't always stick with your tried and trusted team and format. Encourage new talent, too.

SIGN UP FOR SPORT! DO YOU PLAY IN A SCHOOL OR LOCAL SPORTS TEAM, OR DANCE GROUP? HOW ABOUT SWIMMING LIKE GABRIELLA OR TRY A DRY SKI SLOPE! MEET SOME PALS AND GET FIT!

GET FIT FOR THE GAME!

Get into the habit of warming up before you play sport, whether it's a match or practice session – it will make you fitter and help you to play better, and you are less likely to be injured. Don't be embarrassed – ask your coach to give you some tips, then build up your own routine.

ADD UP YOUR SCORES ...

a) true (10) false (0) b) true (10) false (0) c) true (0) false (10) d) true (10) false (0) e) (0) (10)

TOTAL

WHAT DID YOU SCORE?
50: WOW, WHAT TEAM ARE YOU IN? YOU ARE DOING EVERYTHING YOU CAN TO GET FIT OUTSIDE OF YOUR SESSIONS, TOO.
20-40: YOU PROBABLY DO YOUR BEST AT TRAINING, BUT IMPROVE YOUR FITNESS BY EATING HEALTHILY AND CREATING YOUR OWN FITNESS ROUTINE.
10-20: ARE YOUR THUMBS YOUR FITTEST PART (FROM TEXTING AND VIDEO GAMES)? GET OFF THAT SOFA!

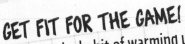

25

GAME ON!

Take away the first letters of the names of each spectator here. Rearrange the letters that are left to find out which Wildcat scores the most baskets in today's match.

M R N K D

J T G T B

D N S O Y

ANSWER: [   ]

HIGH-SCHOOL HERO

It's your turn to try out for the Wildcats!
Can you negotiate your way across the court to shoot?

START

FINISH

HOW LONG DID IT TAKE YOU?
30 SECONDS - WOW. YOU'RE THE NEXT CAPTAIN!
1 MINUTE - GREAT PLAY. YOU'RE ON THE TEAM!
3 MINUTES - A LITTLE PRACTISE AND YOU'LL MAKE THE TEAM!
5 MINUTES PLUS - NEXT!

FIRST OR LAST?

Solve the clues and fit the words in the word wheel.
All the five-letter words share the same first or last
letter. Put the shared letter in the centre circle.

CLUES

1 Chad's nickname for Troy!
2 You do this to get a basket
3 You have your lessons in one
4 Good fashion taste
5 Another word for result
6 Chad has number 8 on his and Troy 14 on his ...
7 Another word for PE
8 You learn how to do this in English lessons!

LOCKER LOGIC!

You're new at East High! Whose locker will you get?
Guess who left these bits behind!

ARE YOU A TEAM PLAYER?

Could you be a captain or even coach, or do you prefer a comfy seat on the bench?

1: The ball comes to you. Do you ...

a) shoot instantly?

b) pass to a player who's in a better position?

c) panic?

2: What is your preferred sport?

a) Basketball

b) Gymnastics

c) Anything played on a Wii.

3: What's your favourite team position?

a) Any position, you like to try them all out.

b) Any position you can shoot in, preferably.

c) In the crowd.

4: When you play, do you usually ...

a) yell orders, to get the game going.

b) play as if a talent scout is watching!

c) try to avoid other people jumping on your toes.

5: The play is up at the other end of the arena. What are you thinking?

a) It'll soon be time for a break and a snack!

b) You're calculating the seconds until the ball reaches you!

c) Wondering what you should do to improve your stamina?

6: How good are you at warming up?

a) Well, you do a bit of a run.

b) You warm up during the game.

c) Great – it's important, so you lead the team in stretches.

Mostly Greens – You love sport and you're very fit, but you don't always work for the good of the whole team. You would excel at an individual sport such as athletics, swimming or tennis, but try and take note of what your team-mates are doing in group games!

Mostly Reds – You are most definitely a team player and are probably captain already! You always have the team's interests at heart, rather than just going all out for glory! Make sure you're not too bossy, and you'll be popular, too!

Mostly Blues – Come on, make an effort! You might be surprised and discover how much you like it! Team sports such as baseball or cheerleading can be great fun and good exercise, or why not try something more unusual like climbing? Find your thing!

28

CHAD DANFORTH:

EAST HIGH HIGHLIGHTS

Chad has so enjoyed his life at East High – it's almost like one big highlight! Most of the magical moments that stand out for him involve basketball! He helped lead the Wildcats to State Championships two years in a row.

GO WILDCATS!

The Wildcats are like Chad's family. He is always there for them and can fire them to victory as co-captain with Troy – his best friend since they were at pre-school. Through Troy, Chad also discovered that braniacs can be cool too – especially Taylor! By getting to know Chad, Taylor realised that sporty guys didn't leave their brains on the basketball court!

Stunning on stage!

Who would have thought that Chad would ever be dancing in a school production? So much for "I don't dance"! His athletic skills and sporty nature make him a natural mover on stage too, with very good timing!

WHAT'S YOUR FAVOURITE CHAD MOMENT AT EAST HIGH?

....

....

....

SPORTING STYLE

LOOK GOOD WHILE BEING A SPORTS STAR!

Find out how to grab attention on court!

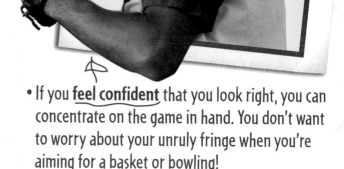

• **Plaits and ponies** are perfect and look cute too!

WINNER
PREPARE YOURSELF BEFORE YOU GO ON COURT. THEN FORGET ABOUT HOW YOU LOOK ONCE YOU HAVE LEFT THE DRESSING ROOM!

• If you **feel confident** that you look right, you can concentrate on the game in hand. You don't want to worry about your unruly fringe when you're aiming for a basket or bowling!

• **Short** haircuts like Zeke's are top for budding sports stars and easy to care for, too! But they don't suit everyone. You shouldn't have to choose your sport over your hair! Chad has one of the biggest hairdos around and is ace at sport. He keeps it back with a headband or under a hat.

• **Keep your outfits simple** and comfy. Not too tight to move and not so baggy they slip down when you run!

Sharpay proves that sports outfits don't have to be grey, shapeless and made of flannel! She brings a touch of drama to any sports field. Don't forget to co-ordinate with **little gloves, sweatbands and colourful trainers**. With a bit of luck, spectators will be so struck by your dress sense they won't see you miss the ball!

The truly style conscious can choose a sport to suit their wardrobe!

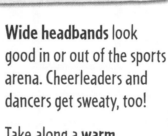

Wide headbands look good in or out of the sports arena. Cheerleaders and dancers get sweaty, too!

Take along a **warm top** to keep you looking cool but feeling cosy while you're waiting for your turn to play!

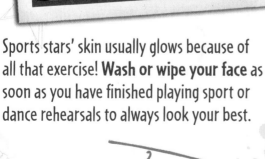

WILDCAT
32

Sports stars' skin usually glows because of all that exercise! **Wash or wipe your face** as soon as you have finished playing sport or dance rehearsals to always look your best.

Troy

Taylor

PLAN AN AWESOME PARTY!

Surprise your pals with a fun party idea! A picnic on a golf course might not be the thing – but plan an impromptu party and get everyone together!

SET THE MOOD!

For an evening garden party (weather allowing!), hang fairy lights or lanterns around the garden. Pop tealights in clean, empty jam jars to create a magical glow. Or go green, and use solar garden lights.

GET WITH THE GAMES!

If you have energetic pals or are worried that people will be bored, throw a games gathering. Go a little old-school and have sack races and a wheelbarrow race! If you're in a park, organise a fun baseball match or design a mad obstacle course using whatever props you have to hand! Activities are great ice breakers and everyone will be laughing together in no time!

Party essential: Have plenty of cooling drinks to hand.

AN EXCUSE FOR A PARTY!

Parties don't have to take months of organising to impress. Why not invite everyone around right now?

Need an excuse? Try one of these!

You have a new recipe to try out, and want to share it ☐

There's a film on TV you just have to see – with friends ☐

You have a new tune to play! ☐

You're having a bad-hair day and need some styling tips! ☐

You've spent ages planning a picnic – and it rains! Never mind, no need to have soggy sarnies – spread out the tablecloth on the floor inside instead!

POP STAR PARTY!

Music makes every party fun. Get a karaoke machine or some tunes and a hairbrush and take turns miming, singing and dancing along.

Invite all the budding stars you know – your best friends, that is!

Dress code: Ask everyone to dress as their favourite pop star or rapper, and you all have to guess who they are!

Snacks: Popcorn.

BEACH BOYS AND GIRLS

Why not plan a beach party ... at home?

Lay out deck chairs or bright beach towels to lounge on.

Dress code: Bright 'n' baggy beach shorts and sun dresses.

Party essential: Sunglasses!

BEACH PARTY SNACKS

• Freeze some fresh fruit juice lollies and hand them out!

• Serve mocktails with juice and fizzy water, decorated with paper parasols!

33

THE FRIEND FILES

How well do you know your friends?
Find out with our Friend-File test!

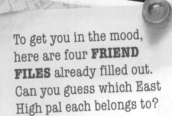

Hand all your friends a piece of paper with the same questions, like my fave film, fave colour, dream destination, secret crush ... Everyone fills in a mini-file then pops it in a box, hat or sock!

Each pal takes turns to read one aloud and you all have to guess whose file it is!

CHOOSE WHATEVER QUESTIONS YOU LIKE, BUT DON'T GET TOO PERSONAL!

DON'T LET ANYONE SEE YOUR FILE AND DON'T WRITE YOUR NAME ON IT!

To get you in the mood, here are four **FRIEND FILES** already filled out. Can you guess which East High pal each belongs to?

 1

FRIEND FILE

My favourite book
The Phantom of the Opera

My kind of film
Musical

Dream holiday
Chilling in Hollywood

Fave food
Chicken and mango salad

Fave animal
Otter

Top colour
Turquoise

WHOSE FILE?

 2

FRIEND FILE

My favourite book
Little Women

My kind of film
Rom-com

Dream holiday
Any beautiful beach

Fave food
Pizza

Fave animal
Koala

Top colour
Peach

WHOSE FILE?

34

DICEY ADVENTURE

Try our fun prediction game!
Think of a question, then roll the dice.
What did you score?

WHAT DID YOU ROLL?

1 You can make it happen – go for it!

2 Is this what you really want?

3 Stop worrying – relax, it won't be as bad as you think!

4 You need to ask that person!

5 Don't expect too much right now!

6 Things will happen – it's up to you to make the most of them.

Stick your own photo here!

3 FRIEND FILE

My favourite book
Madame Curie biography

My kind of film
True-life stories

Dream holiday
Culture break at museums

Fave food
Lasagne

Fave animal
Sea Turtle

Top colour
Midnight blue

WHOSE FILE?

4 FRIEND FILE

My favourite book
To Kill a Mockingbird

My kind of film
Action adventure

Dream holiday
Skiing

Fave food
Cheeseburgers

Fave animal
Wolf

Top colour
Red

WHOSE FILE?

HERE'S ONE FOR YOU TO FILL IN!
MY FILE

What film would I star in?

What song would I sing?

What cartoon character am I most like?

What animal would I be?

Who would play me in the film of my life?

ANSWERS ON PAGE 67

GET COOKING!

If you love cooking, like Zeke, you'll love making these yummy vegetable kebabs. They taste as good as they look!

WHAT YOU NEED
FOR FOUR KEBABS (TWO SERVINGS)

4 skewers (handle with care!)
2 red peppers (chopped into chunks)
2 green peppers (chopped into chunks)
2 small onions (chopped into chunks)
12 button mushrooms (washed)
12 cherry tomatoes (washed)

1 Gather your vegetables together and cut them all into bite-sized chunks. Cut them roughly the same size so they will cook evenly.

2 Carefully push the vegetables on to the skewers in whatever order you like! Stick a tomato on the tip of the skewer to cover the sharp point!

QUICK QUENCHER

Fruit smoothies are a tasty way to quench your thirst. Use fresh or frozen fruit.

For two people you will need:
1 banana – peeled and chopped
2 oranges – peeled
10 strawberries – stalks removed
OR half a glass of frozen raspberries or mixed berries

1. Pull the oranges into segments and put them in a large jug with the banana.

2. Add the strawberries or frozen berries.

3. Whizz the fruit together with a hand-held processor for 2 to 3 minutes until the mixture is thick and smooth.

4. Pour into two glasses, decorate with a strawberry or orange slice and enjoy!

ASK AN ADULT TO HELP WHEN USING SHARP KNIVES AND THE OVEN OR GRILL.

3

Put the kebabs under the grill at a medium temperature until the onions start to go brown and the tomatoes go soft. They are then ready! Serve and eat them straight away!

If you are planning a picnic, **raw vegetable kebabs** are perfect to take along for a colourful and crunchy treat!

Use mini wooden cocktail sticks, and thread each with a chunk of cucumber, a baby tomato and a chunk of red pepper.

Serve them by sticking the cocktail kebabs into a large orange!

CHANGING ROOMS!

Sharpay's dressing room suits a rising star. It's full of her favourite things to create good vibes before she goes on stage. But everything is not perfect – can you spot 10 differences in the bottom picture?

ANSWERS ON PAGE 67

RYAN EVANS:

EAST HIGH HIGHLIGHTS

It's not always easy being Sharpay's twin – Ryan sometimes feels a little overshadowed. On the bright side, having a twin at East High has given him a constant companion and duet partner for the musicals! Ryan has so many fun shows at East High to remember!

Fun and friendships

One of Ryan's best memories of East High life is the summer vacation when the class joined him and Sharpay at Lava Springs! Ryan had both his family and his friends around and discovered that feeling of being part of a team – a firm group of friends – for the first time! Helping his school friends to put on their own show number at the summer camp was a turning point in his school life.

Doing his own thing

Putting on the spring show in Senior Year has to be a true highlight. Choreographing the whole show, and helping with design – Ryan really let his imagination work overtime. Anyway, who else could carry off those outfits?

WHAT'S YOUR TOP MEMORY OF RYAN'S TIME AT EAST HIGH?

....

....

....

GET INTO THE GROOVE

Get together with your pals and try to recreate the fun dance scenes and moves demonstrated by the funky friends at East High!

- Make your dance as showy as you want!
- Remember to move your arms too – don't leave them limply at your side!
- Get co-ordinated with your pals. Try something simple to get started.

- Try stepping forward and to one side with your right foot. Bring the other foot to join it. Repeat that twice, then bend your knees and circle your hips, while moving your right arm forward then to the side as if you're in water – all in perfect timing!
- Add a clap and spin around – make sure you all go in the same direction!
- Take it in turns to add a dance move of your own and become choreographers, like Ryan! It will be a true team effort!

PUT ON A DVD OR CHOOSE SOME TUNES YOU ALL LIKE AND FIND THE RHYTHM!

GET A PARTNER

Partner dances don't have to be slow and smoochy! Hold your partner's hand, move in towards each other, and make gentle high fives in the air. Then move back away again, in time to the music. Add a few twirls if you like!

40

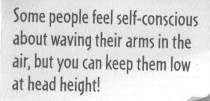

Some people feel self-conscious about waving their arms in the air, but you can keep them low at head height!

FREESTYLE!

There's no right or wrong about dancing – everyone has their own beat. You've just gotta find it! But, once you have found it, try to keep in time!

Crowded dance floor? No worries. Just swing your hips and move your upper body.

Don't think that people are staring at you – they're probably too busy wondering how they look to notice you! Unless you've jumped up on the stage, that is!

Look happy! People will come and join you on the dance floor because you're having such fun!

PRACTISE DANCING IN FRONT OF A MIRROR TO YOUR FAVOURITE TUNES!

DANCE DILEMMA!

Eek! Taylor and Chad have to learn to waltz for the prom! Can you help them to move around the dance floor without stepping on each other?

You have to visit EVERY square – but only once. Step on a boy's shoe and you can move to the next square in any direction EXCEPT DIAGONALLY. If you step on a girl's shoe you can only move diagonally!

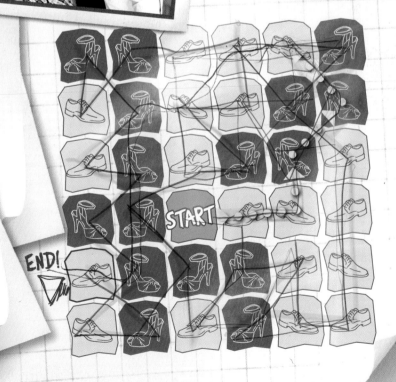

START

END!

ANSWER ON PAGE 68

WHAT'S YOUR KARAOKE STYLE?

The mic is thrust at you – what will you do? Are you a diva like Sharpay? Will you sing a sweet duet like Troy and Gabriella or play piano and sing along Kelsi-style?

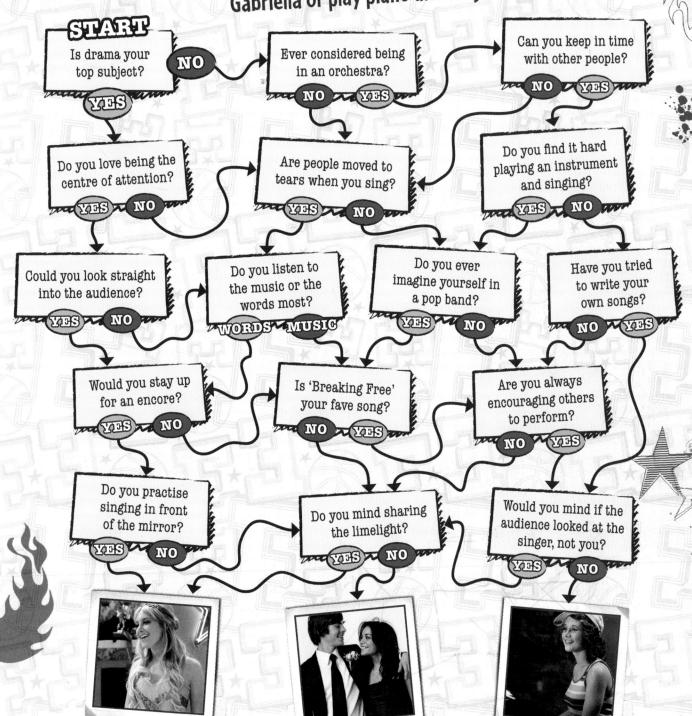

START
Is drama your top subject?
NO · YES

Ever considered being in an orchestra?
NO · YES

Can you keep in time with other people?
NO · YES

Do you love being the centre of attention?
YES · NO

Are people moved to tears when you sing?
YES · NO

Do you find it hard playing an instrument and singing?
YES · NO

Could you look straight into the audience?
YES · NO

Do you listen to the music or the words most?
WORDS · MUSIC

Do you ever imagine yourself in a pop band?
YES · NO

Have you tried to write your own songs?
NO · YES

Would you stay up for an encore?
YES · NO

Is 'Breaking Free' your fave song?
NO · YES

Are you always encouraging others to perform?
NO · YES

Do you practise singing in front of the mirror?
YES · NO

Do you mind sharing the limelight?
YES · NO

Would you mind if the audience looked at the singer, not you?
YES · NO

SOLO SUCCESS
Who needs a band or background dancers – they would just detract from you! Grab that mic and wow the crowd!

IT TAKES TWO!
Having a friend to sing with gives you the confidence to get up on stage. But once you're up there, you'll shine!

PLAY IT AGAIN
You love music and performing, but would rather be seen as a musician, a playmaker even. Try not to hide behind your instrument!

43

SET THE SCENE

CREATING A MOOD

You're all set to star in the school musical – but are you prepared? Will you go O.T.T., like Sharpay and Ryan, with an up-tempo arrangement, colourful costume changes, props – the whole works? Or will you be laid back and natural, like Troy and Gabriella?

SPECIAL EFFECTS

Balloons, stars, tinsel and glittery backdrops say celebration and fun. The right decorations can transform a plain stage and create a party atmosphere for the audience. Getting the mood right is important. Choose a costume to suit your background. Your gym gear might look a bit out of place for a scene like this – unless it's glittery, that is!

WHAT FILM CHARACTER WOULD YOU BE?

DRESS IN CHARACTER!

Dressing up as a film or book character can help you relax – you're playing a part, so it's almost like wearing a mask! Besides, if the audience is looking at the whole spectacle, they might not notice if you make a mistake!

EHS

THEMED FEELING

You don't need to decorate the whole stage. If your turn is part of a varied show, then keep it simple. Sharpay and Ryan's tinsel-covered ladder was inspired. Easy to prepare and carry on, and it gave them a focus!

A VISUAL FEAST!

Sharpay and Ryan love to put on a spectacular show! Nothing is left to chance – their outfits are glam, the dancers' costumes are co-ordinated, the scenery is just right, and there are always extra little touches, from falling confetti to fireworks going off around them! It takes a lot of planning and practice to get it perfect, but they wow every time!

STAR TIP!
BE INSPIRED! THINK ABOUT THE KIND OF SHOWS YOU LIKE TO WATCH – AND WHY.

WHAT'S YOUR SHOW STYLE?

WHOSE STYLE?

Can you guess which East High students these items belong to?

EAST HIGH SCHOOL

CLUE: THERE ARE SIX DIFFERENT STUDENTS

SHADOW DANCING

Can you guess the dancers from their silhouettes? CLUE: THESE SNAPS ARE ALL IN THE ANNUAL!

A

B

C

D

ANSWERS ON PAGE 68

SHARPAY EVANS:

EAST HIGH HIGHLIGHTS

Sharpay's fondest memories of East High are of course the times she was on stage – so there are a lot of them! She's played the lead in 17 high-school productions!

In fact she was almost guaranteed the starring role with twin Ryan, until Gabriella and Troy took an interest in the shows!

DAZZLE TIME

But Sharpay recognises talent, and another big thrill was when she rehearsed with Troy for the Midsummer's Night Talent Show during the vacation at her parents' holiday resort. Offstage, Troy helped her to improve her golfing skills!

When not onstage, Sharpay was always organising the next production as co-president of the East High Drama Club.

Sharpay is so used to getting admiring glances, it came as no surprise to see that Zeke, one of the cutest (and tallest) guys on the basketball team, had a little crush on her! He even baked her little treats!

WHAT'S YOUR STARRIEST EAST HIGH MOMENT FOR SHARPAY?

....

....

MAKE A MINI HOOP!

Want to make the Wildcats team? Your training starts here! Turn an empty orange net and some cardboard into a hoop and go for it!

WHAT YOU NEED

- Pencil and paper
- Scissors
- Thick cardboard
- Sticky tape and glue
- Strips of old newspaper
- A satsuma or orange net (empty!)
- Bright red and blue paint
- Paintbrush

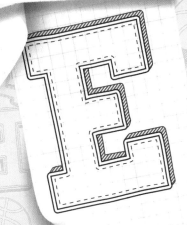

1

Cut a length of cardboard about 7cm wide by 40cm long and fold it over twice. Use sticky tape to hold it together. Wrap strips of newspaper over it, sticking the ends down, then bend it to create a hoop shape.

48

SHOOT!
Find a small, soft ball to throw through your hoop!

TO PLAY!
Bend back the bottom and sides of your backboard and tape or Blu-tak them to a wall or the back of a chair.

4

Push the ends of the hoop through the slit in the centre of your backboard. Use sticky tape to fix the ends firmly at the back of the board. You won't see this, so it doesn't matter if it looks scruffy!

2

Create a backboard. Draw a curved rectangle shape on thick card, with 5cm strips at the sides and a 3cm deep strip at the bottom. These will fold back to stick to a wall. Cut a slit in the centre.

3

Paint your backboard. Use a bold colour and add your team name or copy the East High logo! Paint the paper-covered hoop and let it dry. Hang the net over the hoop and stick it in place at the top.

WHAT DOES YOUR ABOUT YOU?

Next time you scrawl a note or write out some homework, take a little more effort with your handwriting – it could be saying more about you than your words!

Gabriella

MARGINS

Look at your school exercise books.
Do you start writing right by the margin on every line?
Yes? Then you are organised, and like things to be neat, with everything ready for class, parties or after-school activities ...

Or does your writing gradually move away from the margin at the bottom?
Is this you? Then you put off doing things, like homework assignments, learning your lines, and revising, until the last moment!

Or, do you start away from the margin and stay there so there is a gap all round your work?
You like to play it safe and don't like to do things on impulse.

Is the writing more squashed up on the right-hand side and bottom because you seem to run out of room?
Then you are impulsive and don't always think things through properly before you do them!

Troy

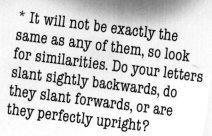

THE WRITE STUFF

Write a short line about yourself. Now look at the samples of writing on the next page and see which one it matches most closely.

_____
_____
_____
_____
_____
_____

* It will not be exactly the same as any of them, so look for similarities. Do your letters slant sightly backwards, do they slant forwards, or are they perfectly upright?

Do your letters slant backwards? Then you are a little bit shy and don't like to show your feelings.

Your letters slant in different directions, but sometimes stay upright. Yes? You are sometimes nervous, a bit unpredictable, and could be a little more organised!

Do your letters slant forward? You look forward to the future with confidence.

Perfectly upright, centred letters You are in control of your life and think about the here and now.

Look at your vowels and the letters with tails. Are they round but joined up? You are open to other people, but good at keeping secrets!

Are the vowels gappy, not quite joined up? Yes? You are a very open person, but find it hard to keep secrets!

Are there lots of loops in your letters? You are quite secretive – you don't reveal a lot about yourself to most people!

Adding stars, smilies and decorations to your signature shows a very confident personality!

Sharpay

It's important to create an individual signature that no one else will copy and that friends will recognise as your own!

Create your own unique signature here!

My signature:

Date:

Writing your signature in CAPS means you like to stand out!

CHAD

Troy

SUPER SENIOR-YEAR SQUARE

Immerse yourself in everything at East High and see what you can find in our shockingly big wordsearch. There is one word you won't find! Which is it?

Word list:
- BASKETBALL
- CANTEEN
- CHAD
- CHEERLEADERS
- CHEMISTRY
- COOKING
- DANCE
- DRAMA
- FRIENDS
- GABRIELLA
- MARTHA
- MUSICAL
- PARTIES
- PLAYMAKER
- PROM
- REHEARSAL
- RYAN
- SCHOLARSHIP
- SENIOR YEAR
- SHARPAY
- SINGING
- TAYLOR
- TEAM
- THE ROCKET
- TIARA
- TROY
- WILDCATS
- YEAR BOOK
- ZEKE

Grid:

```
G S B R I E N D S F R G U W R
Z E N T E K C O R E H T E L G
N N E E T N A C H A W N A B A
N N E E T N A C H A W N A B A
S I N G I N G E D O H C R H I
R O L Y A T A R A L I L T A A
T R C J X R B U T S L R R L C
P Y A A S K R S U S A N O B O
I E N A S A I M U M G A B Y O
H A L I H M E Y E A R B O O K
S R E D A E L R E E H C U B I
R L E A R B L R B S C P Z Y N
A N L N P L A Y M A K E R N G
L P A R A I T S T N E N O Z
O I R I Y I D T K K Z I K I M
H A N O Y N C A W E C N A D A
C G R T E E O C T L T E A M T
S T B I K O N D N S D B M N Y
O I R E O G T L U I A N A Y R
Y F Z Y R T S I M E H C R L
B Y E L R A M W Z H C S D F L
```

ANSWERS ON PAGE 68

52

TAYLOR McKESSIE:

EAST HIGH HIGHLIGHTS

Taylor really made the most of her time at East High – no one knows how she did it all! She was president of the Chemistry Club, a member of the East High National Honor society and captain of the Scholastic Decathlon. And she always made time for her best friends – Gabriella Montez and Chad Danforth!

Amazingly, she even went to see Wildcats basketball matches, despite once thinking that the student athletes were a little academically challenged!

Taylor has had a brilliant opportunity to recap her Senior Year while putting together the East High Year Book. Yup, she even found time to edit that!

Biggest highlight?
Captaining the winning team at the Scholastic Decathlon – against true rivals, West High! On another level, Gabriella coming to East High! It was the start of a true close friendship, someone who felt the same, and who helped Taylor to see outside her close circle.

WHAT DO YOU REMEMBER MOST ABOUT TAYLOR'S TIME AT EAST HIGH?

....

....

....

CAN YOU SURVIVE EAST HIGH?

Grab some pals and share the pitfalls and highlights of life at East High. Tread carefully through your final years and see whether you are first to graduate in style!

You will need:
- A dice
- Some counters (Buttons or charms will do, or make some cool counters from card by copying this template!)

DRAW A TROPHY ON CARD WITH AN EXTRA 1-2CM OF CARD AT THE BOTTOM TO BEND BACK SO IT STANDS UP! MAKE ONE FOR EVERY PLAYER!

© Disney

START!

You're caught chatting in class and get a detention. Miss a turn!

THROW A FIVE TO MOVE ON!

Oops, you forget your lines at rehearsal. Go back 3 spaces!

TAKE AN EXTRA TURN!

You score the deciding basket in the match! Have another go!

THROW A SIX TO MOVE ON!

TAKE AN EXTRA TURN!

You have NOTHING to wear to the prom! Miss a turn while you shop!

Top marks in maths! Double your dice score!

TAKE AN EXTRA TURN!

You wow at rehearsals – go forward 2 spaces!

You're out of hair gel on prom night. Throw the exact number to finish!

Yay! You make the basketball team! Go forward 3 spaces!

THROW A FIVE TO MOVE ON!

BACK YOU GO!

Finish!

YOU MADE IT!

TAKE THE LONG WAY!

IF YOU LAND ON THIS SQUARE YOU HAVE TO FOLLOW THE ARROW!

Guess who's singing out of key? Go back 4 spaces!

THROW A SIX TO MOVE ON!

TAKE AN EXTRA TURN!

You freeze in your audition for the musical. Go back 5 spaces!

Remembering those dance moves is tricky. Miss a go to practise!

TAKE THE SHORTCUT!

TAKE THE QUICK ROUTE ONLY IF YOU LAND ON THIS SQUARE

EAST HIGH

POLISH UP FOR PROM NIGHT!

Going to a prom is a bit like performing on stage – you have to dress up, look the part and make an entrance! Follow our essential advice and you too will look your best for the school 'do'!

WHO'S THAT GIRL?

Proms provide the perfect place to **really dress up**! You may not get the chance again for a very long time, so make the most of it! Pick something you would never usually wear. You will be **amazed** at how different you look – and so will everyone else!

DRESSING UP TIME!

Experiment! Try on a few **completely different** styles before choosing. Chad's suit here is way dressier than his gym clothes, but it's still more funky than formal!

Getting ready together can be like a **pre-prom party**! You can help each other into your clothes, give advice on hair and accessories, sing or tell jokes! You'll all feel more relaxed!

Go **shopping** with your pals! Shopping for formal clothes and things you don't often wear can be daunting – so **make it fun**! You will be able to tell by the look on your friends' faces if your tuxedo or dress doesn't look right – and they'll be the first to say you look fab! Just try not to pick the same clothes!

SHIRTS AND TIES!

* Go for a bow or a normal tie? It's all down to you and your shirt! Remember to do up the top button!

* Wear a plain shirt if you have a pattern in your suit.

* Choose a plain suit and you can choose a busy shirt.

* Tuck your shirt in! No letting it hang loose and open on prom night, please!

WHAT'S ALL THIS ABOUT BOYS WEARING FLOWERS?

It's called a corsage! Boys and girls wear them at formal dos, weddings, posh parties and, of course, prom nights.

LEGS HAVE IT!

Prom suits don't have to be black or dark.

Trouser legs can be slim fitting, like Troy's here, or a loose and baggier cut, like Jason's.

IT'S A SHOE THING!

No, **you cannot wear trainers** with a suit. End of story! Look for some soft black shoes that will feel comfy.

Girls have an easier time. If you're used to heels, try some strappy ones, but remember you need to walk and dance and get home at the end of the evening! You can always wear sparkly or velvet pumps.

THE LONG AND THE SHORT OF IT!

Long dresses look **glam**, but not if you are likely to tread on the bottom and trip! The only firm rule with all prom and party clothes is to feel good, and be able to move and dance freely!

STARSCOPES

Is success written in the stars? See what your star sign says!

ARIES
The Ram March 21 – April 20

Aries people are in a hurry to get to the top! Ambitious and very competitive, you have what it takes to succeed, but try not to rush ahead without thinking. And don't get impatient if things don't go as planned!

GEMINI
The Twins May 22 – June 20

Gemini peeps are lively, talkative, popular and confident – natural entertainers! Your jokey nature sometimes hides nervousness and you're a bit forgetful! So practise, then relax and enjoy the attention!

TAURUS
The Bull April 21 – May 21

Patient and practical, you're quietly determined to succeed, but you are realistic. You can be a bit lazy, but once you decide on a goal, you will work hard to get it! Go on, put yourself out more!

CANCER
The Crab June 21 – July 23

You are artistic and imaginative and can be a little moody! You like little luxuries, a comfy family life, and you like friends to approve of what you do. Be daring – if your friends don't want to do something you do, go along anyway, it will be fun!

LEO
The Lion July 24 – August 23

Leos love to be centre stage and want to be noticed! You also want to be liked and are generous and kind to your friends! Sometimes you are afraid to ask for help, but show you are human and people will love you all the more!

VIRGO
The Maiden
August 24 – September 23

You are trusting, funny, quick witted, practical and have very good taste with a great sense of style! You're also a bit of a perfectionist. Try to be a little less fussy and you'll reach your goals!

SCORPIO
The Scorpion
October 24 – November 22

You are strong-willed and like to be in control of your life – so you can be a bit argumentative! You can be mysterious and secretive – why not tell friends your dreams? Others might share your passions!

SAGITTARIUS
The Archer
November 23 – December 21

You can be bold and adventurous. You're always making big plans, but are cheerful and generous if all falls through. Keep going, you never know what's around the corner!

LIBRA
The Scales September 24 – October 23

You are peace loving, friendly and fair and good at getting people together. You're happy to join in events, sports or shows, but often do things to please others! Try to please yourself sometimes!

CAPRICORN
The Goat
December 22 – January20

You have big goals and you're not afraid to work hard for them. You can be a little shy and scared to join in. Have more faith in yourself and go for gold – it's within your reach!

AQUARIUS
The Water Carrier
January 21 – February 19

You like to be different and to shock people with your ideas! You can be a bit materialistic, so remember that friends are more important than riches and you'll be happy as well as successful!

PISCES
The Fish February 20 – March 20

Pisces peeps are dreamers! You are sensitive, creative and caring, but you can be restless, stubborn and a bit over-dramatic! Try to think what you really want and you can make it happen!

59

BIG QUIZ

It's time to test your High School Musical knowledge again ... good luck!

1 What's the first song the Wildcats sing in High School Musical 2?
a) Breaking Free
b) What time is it?
c) All for One   Answer ☐

2 What style of dance does Martha ask to work into the show?
a) Break dance
b) Hip Hop
c) Clogging   Answer ☐

3 Where is Tiara Gold from?
a) London
b) Los Angeles
c) Sydney   Answer ☐

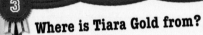

4 Where does Zeke attend college?
a) Cornell University
b) The University of Albuquerque
c) Stanford University   Answer ☐

5 Who sneezes on stage during the performance of 'Senior Year'?
a) Gabriella
b) Troy
c) Sharpay   Answer ☐

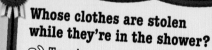

6 Whose clothes are stolen while they're in the shower?
a) Troy's and Chad's
b) Chad's and Zeke's
c) Jimmie's and Donny's   Answer ☐

7 What does Chad say Sharpay should take up after she hits a golf ball right past his head?
a) Baseball
b) Knitting
c) Cooking   Answer ☐

8 What is Chad saving up for with his summer job earnings?
a) An apartment
b) A car
c) College   Answer ☐

9 What does Sharpay have an allergic reaction to during the show?
a) Her dog
b) Jimmie's cologne
c) Dust   Answer ☐

10 The award for winning the Midsummer's Night Talent show is called ...
a) The Star Dazzle Award
b) The Razzle Dazzle Award
c) The Dazzler Award   Answer ☐

1 Where does the song 'The Boys are Back' take place?
a) A car park
b) A junk yard
c) The basketball court

Answer ☐

12 Who does Ryan ask to Prom?
a) Taylor
b) Ms. Darbus
c) Kelsi

Answer ☐

13 Who are the captains of the Wildcats team?
a) Troy and Coach Bolton
b) Troy and Chad
c) Troy and Jimmie Zara

Answer ☐

14 What 'school' was Tiara at before East High?
a) Cambridge
b) London Academy of Dramatic Arts
c) The Brits

Answer ☐

15 Which University does Gabriella go to for her honours programme?
a) Yale
b) Oxford
c) Stanford

Answer ☐

16 What is Jimmie Zara's nickname?
a) The Tiger
b) Babe Magnet
c) The Rocket

Answer ☐

17 What does Sharpay like to drink at break?
a) Non-fat, no foam, soy latte with one packet of sweetener
b) Cappuccino with chocolate sprinkles and one sugar
c) Fresh strawberry milkshake

Answer ☐

18 What was the first musical performance called?
a) Twinkle Towne
b) Hollywood High
c) Off Broadway

Answer ☐

19 Who scores the winning shot of the championship game?
a) Jimmie Zara
b) Chad
c) Troy

Answer ☐

20 What kind of pizza does Troy bring Gabriella for a surprise Senior Year picnic?
a) Margherita
b) Pepperoni
c) Hawaiian surprise

Answer ☐

61

ANSWERS ON PAGE 68

GRAND FINALE

THE SHOW MUST GO ON!

It's opening night for the Spring Musical! But all does not run smoothly. Chaos breaks out and it's down to you and the East High students to save the show.

THE UNDERSTUDY IS – YOU!

It's something you have dreamed of happening, getting to play the lead role, but when the dream comes true, will you panic? Of course not!

COULD YOU GO ON AS UNDERSTUDY AT THE LAST MINUTE?

YES ◯ NO ◯

MAKE THE PART YOUR OWN

Unless you have been given directions to follow, you can play the part in your own way. You don't have to copy the usual actor! Your voice may not be the same as theirs, so rather than struggle to keep high notes, sing it in your own style.

BE TACTFUL!

You may be stepping into someone's shoes, but don't step on their toes, especially if the star is ill. You may think you're better but never, ever, say it!

STAR TIP!
TAKE A DEEP BREATH AND VISUALISE YOURSELF ON STAGE!

STAGE FRIGHT!

Even top actors get stage fright sometimes! Some have been known to go cold and forget their lines on their 50th performance of the same play! Someone will usually whisper the line to prompt you; if not, you might have to 'ad lib' – make something up that could sound likely. Don't worry! What would your teacher prefer – you making up lines, or a long silence?

EH

NIGHTMARE!

You might not have Jimmie the Rocket and his dodgy aftershave near you, but you could have a sneezing fit as you walk on!

What to do? Don't panic! If there's music playing, move in time to the music to face away from the audience (or just turn gracefully) and sneeze through it! Hopefully your cast will notice and step in to help!

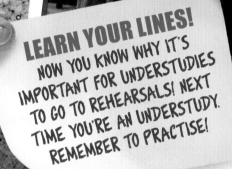

LEARN YOUR LINES!

NOW YOU KNOW WHY IT'S IMPORTANT FOR UNDERSTUDIES TO GO TO REHEARSALS! NEXT TIME YOU'RE AN UNDERSTUDY, REMEMBER TO PRACTISE!

WHERE'S MY MUM ...

Yikes! The theatre looks very different on show nights to when you see it at rehearsals. It's full of people and they are all staring at you! So, lucky you, enjoy the experience!

Look at your stage partner or peer towards the back of the theatre and you won't be able to make out the individuals! Or, if your parents are in the audience, look towards them and imagine you are showing off just to them!

HAVE FUN!

Make the most of your opportunity – you might not get another chance like this! You could be back in the wings tomorrow night, so show everyone what you can really do!

WHOSE ROLE WOULD YOU LIKE TO PLAY?

EAST HIGH SCHOOL

BUDDING BRAINIACS?

Are you are bright enough to get a place on the Scholastic Decathlon team?
Try our teasers and find out. It's testing time!

CRAFTY CONNECTIONS

Can you turn these pairs of words into two
new words by adding a letter in the middle?

CROW [N] EVER

PIN [ ] NEW

HIS [ ] HOW

MEAN [ ] OWN

SEA [ ] OUR

SHIN [ ] EAR

TEA [ ] ATE

EVE [ ] EACH

Add a new word to the start or end of these groups of words to create a longer one!

OUT
SEA → [ ][ ][ ][ ]
BE

[ ][ ][ ][ ] ← FISH
JUMP
LIGHT

[ ][ ][ ] ← SPOT
SHINE
SCREEN

DIRT
TRAIN → [ ][ ][ ][ ][ ]
RACE

[ ][ ][ ][ ] ← FALL
MAN
BALL

TRAINER TRACK!

You see a fab pair of trainers in a sale. Great! But work out exactly how
much of a bargain they really are before you splurge your savings.
The trainers cost £24 at sale price and there is 20% off the original price.
How much would the shoes sell for normally?

a) £27
b) £28.80
c) £30

ANSWER: [ ]

WILDCATS

HOW MANY QUESTIONS DID YOU GET RIGHT?
ALL CORRECT? GRADE A - AS IN A PERFECT STUDENT!
UP TO 3 WRONG: GRADE B - BETTER THAN A LOT OF PEOPLE!
4-6 WRONG: GRADE C - COME ALONG NOW!
MORE THAN 6 WRONG: GRADE D - DARE YOU TRY HARDER?!

ANSWERS ON PAGE 68

WHAT COLLEGE COURSE IS FOR YOU?

Follow the career paths to find where you should head. Is it stage school, a sports scholarship, a catering college or a top university like Gabriella and Taylor?

START

Are you top of the class? — NO / YES

Do you belong to a lot of after-school clubs? — NO / YES

Are you creative? — YES / NO

Trainers or shoes? — SHOES / TRAINERS

Would you try peer tutoring? — YES / NO

Are you good at remembering things? — YES / NO

Do you prefer practical subjects? — NO / YES

Do you guess the ingredients of tasty dishes? — YES / NO

Have you ever turned up to class without a book or pen? — NO / YES

Do you ever make your own lunch? — NO / YES

Are you super-efficient and organised? — YES / NO

Do you dream of being famous? — YES / NO

Do you work best in a team? — NO / YES

Are you fit? — NO / YES

Do you get detention a lot? — NO / YES

Would you mind looking ugly for a role? — NO / YES

How do you feel about wearing an apron? — NO / YES

Have you ever turned up to PE without your kit? — YES / NO

ACADEMIA
You are smart, have a thirst for knowledge and put a lot of effort into your school work. You would enjoy university life.

STAGE SCHOOL
Your heart's set on the stage! You work hard at the subjects you enjoy and would revise to learn your lines, but an office isn't for you.

CATERING COLLEGE
Your creative nature and ability to get on with practical projects combined with a love of food is just like Zeke!

SPORTS SCHOLARSHIP
You wouldn't cope without sport in your life, and why should you? Keep in the game while studying and take it from there!

65

THE FUTURE IS A BIG PLACE!

Ready to take the next huge step? Find out what's in store for the East High crew. Remember, the world is one big stage!

RYAN
The Juilliard School,
Choreography

GABRIELLA
Stanford University,
School of Law

SHARPAY
University of Albuquerque,
Dramatic Arts – and Drama
tutor at East High!

CHAD
University of
Albuquerque,
Basketball

TAYLOR
Yale University,
Political Science

"STEP INTO THE
FUTURE BUT HOLD
ON TO THE PAST"

TROY
University of California,
Berkeley, Theatre
Studies and Basketball

66

KELSI
The Juilliard School,
Music

E
H
S

ANSWERS

P10 T-SHIRT TANGLE
1. Basketball 2. First Aid 3. Chemistry 4. Drama
5. Cheerleading 6. Cooking

Banner reads: Wildcats have sixteen minutes to win!

P14 STEP UP!
1. Gabriella 2. Chad 3. Troy 4. Gabriella 5. Sharpay
6. Taylor 7. Ryan

WORDY WONDER!
TROY › TRAY › TRAP ›TRIP › GRIP › GRIN › GRAN

D.I.Y. WORD LADDERS
SMILE› STILE › STALE › STAGE

P16-17 WHADDAYA KNOW?
1c, 2b, 3a, 4a, 5a, 6b, 7c, 8a, 9c, 10b, 11b, 12b, 13b

P18 CRAZY CROSSWORD!

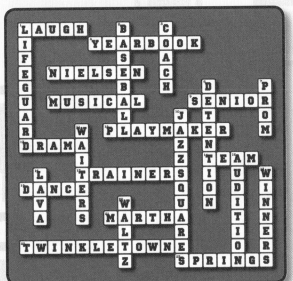

P26-27 GAME ON!
Donny

HIGH-SCHOOL HERO

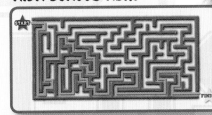

FIRST OR LAST?

LOCKER LOGIC!
a) Chad b) Troy c) Martha
d) Zeke e) Ryan f) Sharpay

P34-35 THE FRIEND FILES
1. Ryan 2. Gabriella 3. Taylor 4. Troy

P38 CHANGING ROOMS!

67

P41 DANCE DILEMMA!

P42 SAY THAT AGAIN!
1. Zeke 2. Taylor 3. Tiara 4. Troy 5. Mr. Fulton
6. Mr. Evans 7. Sharpay 8. Gabriella 9. Chad
10. Chad

P46 WHOSE STYLE?
1. Jimmie 2. Taylor 3. Kelsi 4. Sharpay
5. Ryan 6. Ryan 7. Gabriella

SHADOW DANCING
a) Kelsi b) Chad c) Gabriella d) Sharpay

P52 SUPER SENIOR-YEAR SQUARE
The missing word is: Parties

P60 BIG QUIZ
1b, 2c, 3a, 4a, 5c, 6c, 7b, 8b, 9b, 10a,
11b, 12c, 13b, 14b, 15c, 16c, 17a, 18a, 19a, 20a

P64 BUDDING BRAINIACS?
CRAFTY CONNECTIONS
PinK Knew, HisS Show, MeanT Town, SeaT Tour,
ShinY Year, TeaM Mate, EveR Reach

Side, Star, Track, Sun, Snow

TRAINER TRACK
The trainers were £30 (£24 = 80 per cent;
20 per cent off is £6, 30 minus 6 = 24)

ALL ☆ ABOUT ME

Start planning for college now!

NAME:

AGE: DATE OF BIRTH:

PLACE OF BIRTH:

WHAT I AM GOOD AT:

CLUBS I BELONG TO ...

AT SCHOOL:

OUTSIDE SCHOOL:

SPORTS PLAYED:

MUSICAL SKILLS:

STICK YOUR
PIC IN HERE!

STICK YOUR
HOBBY OR
SPORTING PIC
IN HERE!

Use this space to write why

you think you will succeed!